What Others are Saying about **Picture Perfect**

"*Julie Hedenborg shares her heart in such a way that you will feel understood for the first time. Her vulnerable yet humorous stories make you wish you were a fly on the wall so you can hug her to say you'll laugh at this later. She tackles topics that every mom is challenged by and gives practical advice and encouragement. Every page resounds with the love for Jesus and the Scriptures to support you on your journey of an imperfect but made in God's image mother.*"
— Jill Monaco of Jill Monaco Ministries

"*Real. Raw. Honest. Encouraging. Julie Hedenborg's book, Picture Perfect, feels like a hug for the weary soul! Julie has walked the walk of experience with Jesus and has the healed scars from her blistered feet to prove it. Friend, this book is the salve you've been praying for AND is a MUST READ!*" — Rev. Lori Clifton, Life Strategist & Author of *Transformed: The Journey from Despair to Extreme Hope* and *Love and Other Four-Letter Words*

"*Picture Perfect is powerfully packed with life-saving encouragement for women today. Julie vets out the fluff and writes with focus and purpose in each section, staying on topic for what's most important. I absolutely loved this book!*" — Kathy Burke, Author of *Imagine Heaven Devotional* and *Co-founder, Gateway Church Austin*

Picture *Perfect*

One Mom's Journey from Striving to Finding Her Identity in Christ

A Small Book with a Big, Loving Message for Moms

Julie Hedenborg

Picture *Perfect*

One Mom's Journey from Striving to Finding Her Identity in Christ

Copyright © 2022 Julie Hedenborg

Holy Bible, New Living Translation, Copyright © 1996, 2004, 2015 by Tyndale House Foundation. Used by permission of Tyndale House Publishers, Inc., Carol Stream, Illinois 60188. All rights reserved. Scripture quotations marked TPT are from The Passion Translation®. Copyright © 2017, 2018, 2020 by Passion & Fire Ministries, Inc. Used by permission. All rights reserved. ThePassionTranslation.com.

Publisher: SpeakTruth Media Group LLC, PO Box 1448, Crockett TX 75835

Cover Design: Julie Hedenborg

Photo credits, front: Lindsay Hart and back: Michelle Cichelli of Angel Eye Portraits

Inquiries: order@speaktruthmedia.com

ISBNs:
979-8-9857296-5-8 *(pb)*
979-8-9857296-6-5 *(hc)*
979-8-9857296-7-2 *(eb)*

Printed in the USA
a SpeakTruth Media Book

DEDICATION

> "I actually try and distance myself from school and people because I can't handle the fact that I might be a failure as a mother." — Anonymous

This book is dedicated to a certain mom-friend who texted me last year, along with others like her, who have lost sight of how unique and marvelous they are. I want to remind you that you are created by a God who loves you deeply, SEES you, and has a purpose for you.

CONTENTS

ACKNOWLEDGMENTS

I thank God that I am still here and for giving me another chance to share His goodness and love with others.

To my loving and incredible husband Lars, who supported me in writing this book. You encouraged me to share what God put on my heart. I can't imagine life without you. You inspire me every single day.

To my mom, who taught me to respect all living things and to do my best. I know having me at a young age, you had to forego other dreams and opportunities. Thanks for loving me, making those sacrifices, and being a supportive mother.

To Anders and Kendal, you have my heart. You are two of God's greatest blessings in my life. Thank you for making me a mother, for loving me, and for teaching me so much about life and myself.

Thanks to every friend who hosted a Bible study when it may not have been convenient (Emily, Natascha, Shannon, Heather, Alisha, Selina, Regina). Thanks to my cousin Melanie Clark, who prayed for my family when our faith was weak. I am grateful for every prayer you have prayed for us. Any fruit of my efforts comes back to your faithfulness.

To the chiropractor, who will remain anonymous, thank you. It took me a long time to say this, but I am grateful for what happened because it led me to surrender fully to my Savior. It taught me forgiveness and helped me appreciate each day as a gift. It led me to the podcast, where I have been blessed to hear the most beautiful miracles and meet amazing people. God has used it in ways I could have never imagined. But that is what He does.

To Charlana, I don't know if it would have happened without you, and I thank you for your patience, encouragement, and support.

"We can rejoice, too, when we run into problems and trials, for we know they help us develop endurance. And endurance develops strength of character, and character strengthens our confident hope of salvation. And this hope will not lead to disappointment." Romans 5:3-5 (NLT)

INTRODUCTION

Who Am I and Why Write a Book for Moms?

My name is Julie Hedenborg, and I am a lover of Jesus, a wife, a mom of two, and a former Certified Registered Nurse Anesthetist (CRNA). In 2015 I experienced a life-threatening injury to my neck and a few hardships and undeserved miracles in the process. Ultimately this challenging year changed my life for the better. As a result, I currently host a Christian podcast where I share miracles and testimonies. I can no longer work as an anesthesia provider due to severe scoliosis, but I prefer the term "redirected" over "disabled."

One of the areas of growth for me in this "mom and faith" journey is how different things can be for each of us when we fully surrender to Jesus and realize our identity in Him. I recognize many mothers around me experiencing struggles like my own, and I want to encourage them. While I hope you can find some of my personal stories entertaining and relatable, my true goal is that you can see yourself through God's eyes and have a personal relationship with Jesus and embrace the Biblical truths about your value and worth.

Second to the God piece, I have 22 years of experience in nursing and a Master of Science degree. I love learning about the brain and behavior. I am married to a hard-charging man who works as a business coach. I have been his guest at nearly all the personal development coaching programs (Tony Robbins, Brendon Burchard, Michael Hyatt, and more), and I have heard more lectures on health and behavior than I can count.

I loved seeing psychiatrist Dr. Amen speak live, and I was blessed to be a patient of his Atlanta clinic as well. With all this knowledge, I guess I should be a master of everything, but I am very much a work in progress. I am excited to share some simple things I have learned that can hopefully help others. In short, I have a passion for science, and I love seeing how it ties into God's word, which I will share with *you* in this book.

A Fun Tradition Morphs into Unhealthy Obsession

"Julie, you always have the perfect, most beautiful family Christmas cards," exclaimed sweet Nurse Maureen with her smiling eyes practically beaming heart emojis. If you didn't know her, you might think she was fake, but she is truly that genuine and kind. I love Maureen. I felt a little pang of fraud deep in my gut. "Oh, if you only knew," I replied as we moved our sleepy patient back to her stretcher. I had to confess to her the desperate lengths I have gone to have that picture-perfect image for the annual holiday mass distribution. I secured the best photographer months in advance. Weeks before the session, I would obsess over the perfect color schemes and coordinating outfits. The kids may have a few outfit changes. You can't make them too obviously matchy-matchy, but getting the perfect complementary color scheme is key.

The kids had to be rested and adequately fed with foolproof bribes incorporated into the plan. The typical kid bribe is yogurt with all the sugary toppings or Smarties, candies that don't stain or discolor the teeth. Or the promise of a trip to the trampoline park, anything to get 'er done. I have to say, if the family Christmas card were an Olympic sport, well, I might qualify. The truth of the matter is that obtaining that picture-perfect money shot rests solely on the photographer's talent with editing and filters, lighting, and choosing the right setting.

What Happened in Our 2015 Photo?

BE MERRY!

It was a humid 90-degree fall day in Charlotte as we embarked on capturing our money-shot family photo. I had just returned from Kentucky, where my beloved stepmother had a mastectomy and many more axillary nodes removed than anticipated. The day was stressful as I was still carrying a heavy heart for her and added to that, the summer heat and my continued health concerns. A few months prior, I was transported by ambulance to the Neuro Intensive Care Unit for bilateral vertebral artery dissections, several mini-strokes (transient ischemic attacks or TIAs), and a pseudoaneurysm. I believe this was caused by a manual chiropractic adjustment to my upper neck, although thankfully, I do not have an autopsy report to prove it.

Ultimately, I realized the real enemy was not my chiropractor. What God did in my life was much bigger than the struggle.

I will never forget the casual parting words from the physicians: "You can still have a stroke over the next three months, and *the aneurysm probably won't rupture*. Just call us if you feel like you are having another stroke." All spoken as casually as if we were discussing lunch plans for the next week. As my next CT scan approached, I was dealing with neck pain, overwhelming anxiety, anger, and bitterness. So many questions were floating around in my mind. Would I have to have a stent placed? What if it doesn't heal? What if the aneurysm ruptures? How will I ever find it in my heart to forgive a man who won't even speak to me after what (I believe) he did to my family and me? How do I let go of all this anger and forgive? How long is the neck pain going to last? What if it becomes chronic?

Exhausted from travel, we were not in the mood for a photo shoot, but rescheduling was nearly impossible, so we persevered. I had chosen the location in downtown Charlotte for a more urban feel versus the typical pumpkin patch. There were huge rocks around the park, and the kids were on fire to climb every single one. It wasn't long before meltdowns, literally and figuratively, and my husband Lars was pitting out of his shirt (see the photo here where she added a blanket to the sweat). The kids were fighting, and people laughed loudly while watching the commotion.

Our poor sweet photographer had her work cut out for her.

Fast forward several weeks, my talented photographer friend arrives to share her beautiful work. She miraculously managed to capture a few decent photos, and for fun, she included one she shot from the chaos. We all had a good laugh and kept scrolling to find the money shot. Finally, the day came to compose the Christmas card. Still dealing with so many emotions from all I had been through over the past few months, I started reflecting on the obsessive process of the pursuit of a priceless, perfect photo. Not one photo was jumping out at me other than the outtake photo.

I can't remember why, but I decided the outtake would be the one. I guess part of me felt it was honest. Maybe it resonated with all that I was feeling inside. Maybe it was just a public proclamation to the world, "**I am done**. I am done trying, done striving." After all, who really pays close attention to Christmas cards?

I did it. I sent over 300 cards to the world, to Lars' clients, relatives, school, hospital colleagues, and friends. It wasn't long before the overwhelming responses started to flow. "BEST. CARD. EVER!" was the general reply. One friend said she would frame it and put it out every Christmas! People went nuts over our Christmas card that year. People STILL remember our card from 2015, not the picture-perfect cards that preceded it. Some people even shared their outtakes the next year, and they were great!

Starved for the Authentic

The entire series of events got me thinking. Why such an overwhelming response? In short, I think we are starved for anything authentic. With the advent of social media, I think we have become accustomed to what seems flawless, filtered, and flat-out phony. Even videos can be filtered! I confess I have an application on my phone that I have used a few times to make my eyes brighter, so I am guilty as well. What are we trying to prove, and to whom? I do love the annual cards and updates, but I was beginning to feel ridiculous with the lengths I was going to secure a beautiful card and the value I put on it. I started praying and asking God to show me more insights about myself and anything else He wanted to show me. I began to reflect and see other areas where I allowed my joy, peace, and identity to be sabotaged.

Revelation Sparked by a Christmas Card

I could never have imagined where God would take me and my prayer around my Christmas card. Over some time, I felt God clearly reveal the answers to my questions. He led me to share the message with others who are also struggling. He showed me five major pitfalls that sabotage our identity in Christ: comparison, perfectionism, fear, isolation, and neglect of self-care. Let's take a closer look at each one as they relate to science and Scripture.

MY 5 MOST COMMON PITFALLS

"Your story is unique and so, so different and not worthy of comparison."
— Anonymous.

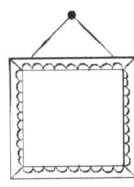

PITFALL #1 – COMPARISON

The Social Media Minefield

We can all agree that social media has become a breeding ground for comparison. Sure, some positive things come from social media, such as the ability to connect worldwide, promote worthwhile causes, and network with people with similar interests. But how does the positive stack up with the negative, and what is the real impact?

I remember a few years back. I met someone who knew my family back home. We hit it off. Let's call her Rachel. We became friends on social media, and I was excited to see her updates as they posted until I wasn't. Rachel's latest smoothie pic perfectly curated with fresh greens and the healthiest additives, then her fun date night posts, girls' weekend away, creative crafts with the kids, fitness challenge posts looking gorgeous, and crushing it at work. Everything so beautiful and polished somehow left me feeling a little envious, left out, and down on myself. I still liked her. I just had these weird emotions as I peered into her seemingly extraordinary life. I noticed her posts stop, and assumed her action-packed life was so full that she no longer had the time to post about it.

When I was home visiting, I asked my dad how she was doing. "She is in jail, honey," replied dad. "WHAT? Rachel? You can't be serious." I replied in complete jaw-dropping shock. "Yes, honey, she has a lot of issues," dad said with quiet compassion. I didn't ask anything else. I share this to point out the amount of power I gave to her posts. Each time I kept seeing them I somehow let it make me feel less than, and it wore at my sense of self-worth. Perhaps it may be more plausible that these perfect posters are struggling and need our prayers the most.

A documentary on Netflix, The Social Dilemma (2020), features tech experts from Silicon Valley, including former employees at Facebook and Google, who have come forward to sound the alarm on the dangers of social media. One disturbing statistic they cited was a 151% increase in suicide rates in girls ages 10 to 14 and a 70% increase in suicide rates in girls 15-19 compared to the average from 2010-2020[1] (social media available on mobile phones 2009). They speak about these platforms being highly addictive and manipulative[1].

In a new study published in the journal Cyberpsychology, Behavior and Social Networking, subjects who took a weeklong break from social media exhibited lower feelings of depression and anxiety. "People who stopped using platforms such as TikTok, Instagram,

Twitter, and Facebook for seven days reported an increased sense of well-being, and some said they freed up about nine hours in their week that they would have spent scrolling[2]." Also, in the article, "Participants who took a break were more likely to agree with well-being statements such as 'I've been feeling optimistic about the future' and 'I've been thinking clearly.' They were also less likely to feel nervous, worried, or report depressive symptoms[2]." (May 6, 2022, Source WebMD, One-Week Social Media Break Reduces Anxiety, Depression by Carolyn Crist.) Results indicated that taking even a week's break from social media can significantly affect mood and clarity! WOW!

One news article published by U.S. News (July 20, 2021) calls social media a public health crisis. Helen Lee Bouygues, founder and president of the Reboot Foundation, writes:

"Earlier this year, the Reboot Foundation, which I run, surveyed more than 1,000 Americans on their social media usage – and we found a disturbing impact on mental health. All this points to how our social media usage has become a **public health crisis**. I believe we need to start treating these platforms like we do cigarettes and alcohol. That means implementing warning labels and age restrictions and conducting better research into the health effects of long-term usage[3]."

Helen continues: "Sound over the top? Then consider that more than half of the people we surveyed acknowledged that their social media use intensified their feelings of anxiety, depression, or loneliness. They also told us that it contributed to their low self-esteem and made it harder for them to concentrate. Yet despite recognizing these deleterious effects, only about a third said they had taken steps to limit their social media use, such as deleting or suspending social media accounts, turning off their phones, or limiting time on their feeds[3]."

She proposes a society-scale digital detox and suggests warning labels, "What if every time you opened Instagram, you first saw a warning label like those found on cigarettes? 'Caution: Social Media May Be Hazardous to Your Mental Health.' Or when you logged into Facebook, you saw this: 'Warning: Facebook may increase feelings of depression or loneliness and suicidal thoughts.'

Or whenever you received a Twitter notification, this came with it: 'Warning: Heavy social media use is linked to higher rates of depression and anxiety[3].'"

Given the statistical findings regarding social media, we simply must be responsible with what we take in and post and must prohibit or equip our kids, as they are particularly vulnerable. It is critical to be aware of what is triggering us, to set responsible time limits if we use social media, and to detox our accounts and fill them with things that inspire and promote health. I am working on this too. Catch yourself in that triggered moment and ask God to reveal what is behind it. Ask Him for help in cleaning up your intake. It is perfectly OK to snooze or unfollow if something is triggering you. Be honest with yourself. If it costs you your peace, delete it from your devices.

In the last scene of the Social Dilemma documentary, the tech experts and the co-creator of the Like Button are asked how they manage their own intake. Some suggestions they list are: turn off all notifications, don't have devices in the bedroom, set firm time limits on screens, work out a time limit for your kids, or don't allow devices at all for your kids. A few of these tech experts have decided their families will not use social media in any amount. Even as I write this, I admit I am struggling to set limits with social media. Writing this book will motivate me to do a digital detox.

When we get to heaven and stand in front of Christ, the number of likes, followers, and filtered selfies is not important. These things can steal our time and joy, and distract us from what is important. Integrity, holiness, and being Christ-like have eternal value.

Another thing I do and see others do regularly is comparing their journey to someone else. As I wrote this book, I chatted with a friend at horse camp. The topic of my podcast pops up, and she mentions that she wants to fulfill whatever plan God has for her, but she has her hands full with a child at home and a struggling relative who just moved in with her. I messaged her later and felt like I had to help her see that she is already in ministry. She may be saving her relative's life with the way she is helping!

"If you want to change the world, go home and love your family." – Mother Teresa

So many of us don't see being a mom, or our work, whatever that may be, as a ministry. God has people in ministry in hair salons, grocery stores, hospitals, and anywhere! Just because we don't have a physical pulpit or platform doesn't mean God isn't doing powerful things through us. Each day we have an opportunity to love people wherever God has us.

Theodore Roosevelt famously said, "Comparison is the thief of joy." It certainly brings jealousy and pride, and it divides us. Friends, this is not what God wants for us! He has created each of us uniquely, in His image. He has a plan for us according to the gifts He has placed in us. Jesus giving His life to save ours is the only validation we will ever need. You are worthy. You are enough. You are loved!

Reflect

Can you think of a time that you struggled with the comparison trap?

_____

_____

_____

_____

_____

Are there specific areas you tend to compare yourself to others? What could be at the root?

_____

_____

_____

_____

_____

What are some of the beautiful unique things God has created in you?

_____

_____

_____

_____

_____

_____

A few Biblical references regarding comparison:

- Galatians 6:4-5, "Pay careful attention to your own work, for then you will get the satisfaction of a job well done, and you won't need to compare yourself to anyone else. For we are each responsible for our own conduct" (NLT).

- James 3:16, "For where jealousy and selfish ambition exist, there you will find disorder and evil of every kind" (NLT).

- Romans 12:2, "Don't copy the behavior and customs of this world, but let God transform you into a new person by changing the way you think. Then you will learn to know God's will for you, which is good and pleasing and perfect" (NLT).

- 2 Corinthians 10:12, "Oh, don't worry; we wouldn't dare say that we are as wonderful as these other men who tell you how important they are! But they are only comparing themselves with each other, using themselves as the standard of measurement. How ignorant!" (NLT).

- Romans 12:6, "In his grace, God has given us different gifts for doing certain things well" (NLT).

PRAYER FOR OVERCOMING COMPARISON

Dear heavenly Father.

Please help me when I am faced with the comparison trap.
Please help me to see myself through Your eyes.
Thank You that You have given each of us unique gifts and
talents. Help me be a humble encourager and grateful for
the many blessings You have provided.
Please fill me with Your joy today.

In Jesus' name. amen.

"We can choose to be perfect and admired or to be real and loved."
— Glennon Doyle

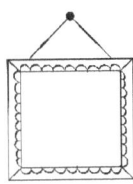

PITFALL #2 – PERFECTIONISM

This is NOT what I expected...

Do you struggle with control issues? Do you frequently set unrealistic expectations for yourself or others?

Being a perfectionist can be a great thing in some respects. For instance, in the meticulous professions who defuse bombs or administer anesthesia. However, perfectionism can also be incredibly detrimental. I am not sure what is at the root of this pitfall for me, maybe fear of not being enough or fear of rejection, but let me tell you, I have allowed an intense desire to be perfect rob me of joy and peace, preventing me from being present with my family. I pray about letting go of my need to be perfect almost daily. I am so grateful that Holy Spirit is close and responds quickly!

Decking the Halls with Mayhem

It was just a few weeks before Christmas and my husband Lars was away. My father-in-law was in an assisted living facility nearby, and I wanted to bring him some Christmas cheer with the kids. He loved Christmas, and I had a grand vision of how we would make his room a winter wonderland, creating a Hallmark moment for all. I purchased a small artificial tree to fit his room, all the décor we could need, dressed the kids in their cute little outfits, and embarked on our memorable journey with visions of sugarplums and the whole nine. My kids were always a much-needed infusion of life in the building, and the residents always lit up with joy as we arrived regardless of my kids' behavior, bulging dirty diapers or decibel levels.

We arrived at Farfar's room (Farfar is Swedish for father's father). He had a private room at the end of the hall, which shared a common anteroom. The roommate never spoke to us, and I was told he was deaf, so I proceeded directly to Farfar to begin the glorious festivities. The kids were super excited and couldn't wait to decorate the tree. Farfar was happy to see us, and soon, we were enjoying the music I brought and opening everything up. It didn't take long before things took a turn. The kids began tossing things all over, fighting over the décor, the brand-new lights somehow got hopelessly tangled, and the kids knocked something over and broke it. Farfar's joy was beginning to dwindle.

My strong-willed child's behavior was escalating. She was overstimulated to the point that I was having a hard time managing her. The pinnacle of the chaos was all around the star. My two kids were screaming like wild howler monkeys, and now the room was in complete disaster. Farfar's face was pale and wide-eyed. He was unable to help me due to his stroke, so he had no choice but to sit back and hope we would leave.

I was getting so frustrated. Holding back my tears, when suddenly the "deaf" roommate emerged at the entryway with an angry red face, hands on his hips, he yelled, "What in the world is going on here??!" I was taken aback as if the resurrected Lazarus was standing before me. I tried to apologize in my best, very sweet, loud voice (even though he was obviously not deaf), hold my tears, restrain my kids, and put the room back together. I apologized to Farfar, managing my emotions until I got back to the car. I cried all the way home at how my sweet sugarplums had turned to hand grenades.

Sadly, I have so many similar stories I could share about my grand visions and expectations. I have finally learned to laugh more when plans fall apart because they will inevitably. As my faith has grown since my injury, I have learned to stop in these moments, look around, and thank God for the things I am grateful for in the middle of the chaos (I promise you that gratitude shifts everything) as I try to see the humor in it.

I have also learned to constantly ask God what HE wants me to see in situations. Is He teaching me something? As I have grown in my relationship with the Lord, these struggles don't disappear. Now I recognize that He is with me in the mess, and He knows my tendencies toward perfectionism and disappointment. He helps me recover so much faster and learn from each one.

You might think it sounds crazy, but sometimes I feel like He is right there and having a little chuckle with me!

Mary and Joseph Lost Jesus for 3 Days[4]

As it relates to perfectionism, there is also such a thing as a righteous comparison. Let me tread lightly here.

Can you imagine how Mary and Joseph must have felt when they lost Jesus for three days? A Pastor spoke recently about how Jesus wasn't lost. He lingered. Either way you slice it, they didn't know where he was. If I had been Mary as my old self, I think my head would have exploded, believing I had lost the one and only Savior of the world. I would have felt responsible for sending the entire world to hell. Perhaps her faith was so solid she had true peace in knowing that Jesus was protected. I don't know, but I just want to thank God for putting that in the Bible. God is truly bigger than anything that can come against us or our perfectly laid or flawed plans!

As a nurse, I feel compelled to say that some cases of perfectionism can require professional help, and it is important to find the right person to help you develop coping skills.

It is time to live more in freedom than the frenzy, to live more present and ditch the obsessive, driven behaviors. After all, the only thing that is truly perfect is Christ and his perfect love for us!

Reflect

Can you recall a time you fell into the trap of perfectionism?

_____

_____

_____

_____

_____

What did it cost you?

_____

_____

_____

_____

What could you do differently to catch yourself in that moment next time?

_____

_____

_____

_____

_____

What the Bible says about perfectionism:

- Matthew 11:28-30, "Come to me, all you who are weary and burdened, and I will give you rest. Take my yoke upon you and learn from me, for I am gentle and humble in heart, and you will find rest for your souls. For my yoke is easy and my burden is light" (NLT). (No striving is needed!)

- Psalms 139:14, "Thank you for making me so wonderfully complex! Your workmanship is marvelous-how well I know it" (NLT). (You are worthy!)

- Romans 15:7, "Therefore, accept each other just as Christ has accepted you so that God will be given glory" (NLT). (Christ already accepts you!)

- Ephesians 2:8-9, "God saved you by His grace when you believed. And you can't take credit for this; it is a gift from God. Salvation is not a reward for the good things we have done, so none of us can boast about it" (NLT). (Salvation is by grace, never earned!)

PRAYER WHEN TEMPTED WITH PERFECTIONISM

Dear heavenly Father.

Thank You for the one truly perfect thing:
YOU (and your Son) and Your love. peace. grace. and mercy.
Please help me when I am tempted to fall into the perfection
trap. Thank You for sacrificing Your only Son so I can live in
freedom and know forgiveness. I want to live with fewer
obsessions and more adoration and trust for You.
Please fill me with Your peace and Your joy today.
Help me to have grace for myself and others. Help me to be
present and aware of the blessings that surround me.

In Jesus' name. amen!

"Feed your faith, and your fears will starve to death."
— Anonymous

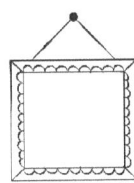

Pitfall #3 — FEAR

What is the opposite of fear? I believe it is faith. I am sad that I didn't have much faith in the early years. I went to church and believed in God, but I had not fully surrendered my life to him. Reflecting on my actions, I didn't trust Him with my kids. Trust the Creator of the universe, the miracle worker who gave his life for me? I somehow believed I could manage them better, which is incredibly hard to admit.

Wow, fear robbed me of so much in my early days as a mother. I am sincerely grateful for the patience God has for me and for the patience my husband has for me, and I am hopeful my kids were too young to realize how much I obsessed over them as babies. Having seen so much trauma in the operating room, I still battle with fear, but I am better about praying and giving it to God.

The Golden Apnea Monitor

Remember, I worked as a Certified Registered Nurse Anesthetist when I had my children. I was an airway expert. I intubated, ventilated, and tracked every cubic centimeter of air moving, every trace of gas in and out of my patient's airway and lungs down to the inert elements. I was so grateful when my colleague Natasha told me I must purchase an apnea monitor for my baby boy. It was the latest and greatest model, with technology that would notify me immediately if my baby stopped breathing (SIDS, Sudden Infant Death Syndrome, was a fear). Of course, I went out to get one and set up the portable crib just outside our bedroom door. I listened to advice from just about every person at the hospital about where to put the baby, which creams and bottles to use, all of it.

Finally, Anders was born, and we had the big first night home. Lars was a saint and set up everything as I asked. We were all set for bed the first night, and we set the glorious gold-plated (in my mind) apnea monitor in just the right place. It wasn't long before Anders awoke with a nearly deafening scream. Imagine your baby screaming in stereo from the door and at full volume from the handset at your ear. Hardly sleeping, we both shot out of bed and nearly trampled each other to get Anders. Lars tried his best to accommodate my specific requests, but finally, he acknowledged how ridiculous it was and moved Anders to the fully equipped nursery down the hall. We finally managed to get a little bit of sleep.

Another obsession I developed was related to my son's diagnosis of hydrocephalus (excess fluid on the brain). My son was born over 10 pounds. Adding this new diagnosis to his size would mean he would hit his developmental milestones late. I devoured everything I could find on development and watched him like a hawk. He didn't walk until he was 17 months. I read all about how critical sleep was, so I had him on a schedule I did not like to break. After all, his life was in my hands. The rigid schedule continued for several years.

"Mommy, I Can't See the Sky!"

My son Anders was around four when we got invited to a New Year's Day afternoon party at the lake on the north side of town. They asked us to arrive around 2 p.m., and I mentally planned out times for feeding/napping my two children and felt it could work. They didn't serve a meal until 7-8 p.m. I was twitching on the inside with the kids' schedules being off. Lars kept reassuring me as I tried to cope. We ended up leaving around 10 p.m. with an hour's drive home. As we were leaving the party, my son walked around to the front of the house and yelled loudly, "Mommy, Daddy! I can't see the sky!" I realized it was the first time my child had ever seen the night sky as he was always in bed before the sunset. We got a laugh out of it and made it home without anyone falling completely apart.

I don't know if I could have been wound any tighter in those early years. If it wasn't SIDS, sleep schedules, snakes in the yard, dry drowning, or protecting my boy from his early peanut allergy, there was always something I was worried about daily. I wish I could have known the peace I could have had if I trusted God. I know bad things happen, and we don't always get a yes answer to our prayers, but when we face it all WITH GOD, it is different. He gives us strength, joy, and a new peace that only comes from Him. Sometimes that comes moment by moment or through leaning on other believers, but if we trust Him, it comes.

Some Interesting Statistics on Chronic Fear

An article from the American Journal of Managed Care (2017), "The Effects of Chronic Fear on a Person's Health," states the potential consequences of fear on overall physical, emotional, environmental, and spiritual health. The effects include:

- Immune system dysfunction
- Endocrine system dysfunction
- Autonomic nervous system alterations
- Sleep/wake cycle disruption
- Eating disorders
- Alterations in the hypothalamus-pituitary-adrenal axis

The potential effects of chronic fear on emotional health include:

- Dissociation from self

- Unable to have loving feelings
- Learned helplessness
- Phobic anxiety
- Mood swings
- Obsessive-compulsive thoughts

The potential consequences of chronic fear on spiritual health:

- Bitterness/fear toward God or others
- Confusion/disgust with God or religion
- Loss of trust in God and/or clergy
- Waiting for God to fix it
- Despair related to a perceived loss of spirituality[5]

Fear is a thief! It robs you of peace, and joy, sometimes sleep, causes strife in relationships, and so much more. Fear is such a common weapon that the enemy uses against us. Your health and destiny are too valuable to allow fear to rob you any longer.

Reflect

What types of fears are pitfalls for you?

_____

_____

_____

_____

What are the costs of those fears?

_____

_____

_____

_____

How can you deal with this next time you feel this trigger?

_____

_____

_____

_____

Surrender your fears to God!

Let Him show you the difference that trusting Him can make.

What does the Bible say about fear? Tons!

- Proverbs 29:25, "Fear and intimidation is a trap that holds you back. But when you place your confidence in the Lord, you will be seated in the high place" (TPT).

- 1 Peter 5:7, "Give all your worries and cares to God, for he cares about you" (NLT).

- Isaiah 41:10, "Don't be afraid, for I am with you. Don't be discouraged, for I am your God. I will strengthen you and help you. I will hold you up with my victorious right hand" (NLT).

- Hebrews 13:5b-6, "For God has said, "I will never fail you. I will never abandon you." So we can say with confidence, "The Lord is my helper, so I will have no fear. What can mere people do to me?" (NLT).

- 2 Timothy 1:7, "For God has not given us a spirit of fear and timidity, but of power, love, and self-discipline" (NLT).

- Psalms 23:4, "Even when I walk through the darkest valley, I will not be afraid, for you are close beside me. Your rod and your staff protect and comfort me" (NLT).

- Deuteronomy 31:6, "So be strong and courageous! Do not be afraid and do not panic before them. For the Lord your God will personally go ahead of you. He will neither fail you nor abandon you" (NLT).

PRAYER WHEN YOU ARE BATTLING FEAR

Dear heavenly Father,

Thank You for being a refuge and a fortress.
You are faithful and can be trusted! Father, please
forgive me for the times I have worried. Lord, help me
not to give in to fear but to remember Your promises.
Help me to be strong and courageous and to know that
You go before me. Thank you. Lord, that You will never
forsake me. Thank You, as I have invited Your Holy Spirit
into my heart, the same power that resurrected Christ
lives in me!

In Jesus' holy and precious name, we pray, amen.

"Hugs are the universal medicine."
— Anonymous

Pitfall #4 – ISOLATION

Isolation is yet another powerful tactic of the enemy. A person can be lonely in a marriage and even around many people. Different things can predispose someone to want to isolate. Guilt, grief, unforgiveness, shame, depression, social anxiety, and unworthiness are a few. According to one report by the National Academy of Sciences, Engineering, and Medicine, social isolation is associated with about a 50% increase in dementia and other serious medical conditions, even premature death![6]

The Power of Human Touch

As humans, we are wired for human connection from birth. I learned as a nurse the dramatic effects of touch on babies, their undeniable connection to the sound of their parents' voices, and skin-to-skin contact immediately after they are born. It is truly a gift to witness this experience with my Cesarean section patients! In anesthesia school, I got so emotional during my first delivery in the operating room that I cried along with the parents. I absolutely loved it. Unfortunately, this day scored me a nickname that stuck for two years, but I won't be sharing that here.

According to a recent article, "The 3 Biggest Advantages of Human Touch May Surprise You," by Sara Menges (Jan 24, 2021)[7], physical touch is a basic human need not just at birth but throughout our lives[7]. We know that touch can stimulate the release of oxytocin, the "feel-good" hormone which helps inspire positive thinking and a generally optimistic outlook. Dopamine and serotonin can also increase to regulate mood and relieve stress and anxiety. Physical touch can also improve the immune response and lower blood pressure. All these things promote physical and emotional wellness!

While most of my life I have been blessed with loving family and friendships, there have been times when I did experience loneliness. I felt lonely in the early days with my newborn, which was probably compounded by the physiological changes happening in my body, grieving parts of my old life, and adjusting to a new life. Today's Parent Magazine reported on a UK survey in March of 2018, further supporting the effects of isolation among new mothers in its article entitled, *"The Excruciating Loneliness of Being a New Mother":*

"A recent UK survey of more than 2,000 mothers by the online mothers' networking group Channel Mums found that 90 percent of mothers feel lonely since having children and 54 percent felt 'friendless' after giving birth. We would do well to pay attention to this phenomenon because long-term loneliness is dangerous. In recent years, it has been linked to increased rates of hypertension, sleep disturbances, and mental illness. According to a UK government report last year, loneliness can be as harmful to your long-term health as smoking 15 cigarettes a day."[8]

We need to check on the new moms we know. Having a baby is a miracle, but it can be a tough transition too.

Bitter, Party of One?

I felt the effects of isolation the greatest after my neck injury in 2015. Initially, I could not drive or work, but only for a few weeks. I did return to work with the clearance of my neurosurgeon. Given that I was still in the period where I could have a stroke, and there was a chance the aneurysm could rupture, I could not, in good conscience, continue providing anesthesia. I guess the risk of those things happening was small if I was cleared to work, but I didn't feel it was fair to my patients. I tearfully submitted my resignation.

I intended to keep a foot in the anesthesia door at places around town, but not long after I quit my hospital job, I would be told I was disabled due to my scoliosis. Losing my healthcare professional community and identity was heartbreaking. These were the people that knew my dating stories, held my wedding and baby showers, and shared daily life with me. We also form strong bonds in this field because of the nature of our work and how we depend on one another in life and death situations. I have kept in touch with a few, but over time people drift apart. I wish it weren't so, but I'm as much responsible for the drifting as anyone else.

Amid all these life-altering, emotional circumstances, I was plagued with anxiety about what might happen to my life. Righteous anger filled my heart for the guy I believed was responsible. I felt completely written off by the entire chiropractic community when I offered to provide my chart and scans for education and research and got no interest. Additionally, I was riddled with guilt that I felt anxious because, medically speaking, apart from the physical pain, I was miraculously free from any residual issues from the dissections. The aneurysm did not heal completely on my last scan, but the surgeon told me it was stable. The pain did take many months to subside, but things could have been SO much worse (death, major stroke, paralysis, chronic pain, etc.[9]). Despite avoiding these horrific outcomes, I was stuck in the injustice, and I became bitter. I wasn't just isolated; I wanted to be alone. I had become a party of one, and I was not fun to be around at all.

Turkey with a Side of Truth

I will never forget when my 5-year-old daughter looked up at me over Thanksgiving dinner with family as I discussed something about my injury. "When are you just going to forgive that man, mommy?" I felt an immediate lump in my throat and silence at the table. It was four months from the incident. Sadly, I didn't fully forgive that man for a year. I knew the Bible said to forgive, and my friend Belinda told me it was simply a decision I had to make. I felt like I was lying to say that aloud, yet still feeling so angry in my heart. I prayed for so long and asked God to help me. I was faithful in praying for the chiropractor, and eventually, God did help me overcome and find closure when He orchestrated our meeting at a gas station.

Divine Appointment at Exxon

"I have fully forgiven him (the chiropractor). I am focusing on trusting God, staying grateful, and finding peace," was my faith-filled text to my Bible study friend on July 27, 2016. Approximately five minutes later, I was standing, in shock, face to face with my chiropractor at a gas station. My heart was beating out of my chest, and my emotions were running high. I didn't know if I would hug him or punch him in the throat, but I prayed. I prayed hard. It was the first time I had seen him since the incident. I spoke from my heart. He invited me to his office to talk, and two days later, we met. It ended beautifully. After a year of so much struggle, I finally had closure.

I will never forget the words he said when I left the office. "We should have had this talk so long ago," he said. "No. I believe this is exactly how it was supposed to be, I understand that now," I smiled with my reply. He added, "You know what is so crazy? I didn't need gas. I had three-quarters of a tank, the light was green, and I have no idea why I stopped at that gas station. It is just crazy that we ran into each other."

God orchestrated that meeting. To this day I don't know if it was a test or a blessing, but with His answer to my plea for help, I consider it a blessing. So many times, we don't get the closure we desperately want, and I feel so blessed to share what God did for me. He can do that for you too. With God's help, I overcame the isolation and bitterness prior to this encounter. It was the icing on the cake I wanted to share with you.

Sometimes God Has Other Plans

Anesthesia was the only thing I had mastered in my life, and I felt it was where I was meant to be. I didn't understand why things turned out the way they did. My job was very stressful, and in some ways, it was a relief not to be working in that environment anymore. It still felt like a monumental loss because I worked so hard to get there.

I stayed isolated for months. In the meantime, Lars' work life was booming. He was in his prime and on-stage hosting coaching events. While I was so happy for him and grateful for his provision for our family, I was still grieving my old identity and community and trying to adjust to my new life as a stay-at-home mom. I felt lost.

God Sends People to Intervene

Carla, who lived in the neighborhood, kept inviting me to her Bible study, but I kept saying no. One day I finally relented so that she would stop asking. Her group was doing Beth Moore's study on The Book of Revelation. I remember thinking to myself, oh joy, the apocalypse! I attended and hardly said a word at first. I didn't feel worthy of being there. I had to locate my Bible, and once I did, it was embarrassing how all the pages stuck together, revealing it was never read. These women were so deep in their faith. God was doing a work through those ladies. Their love and compassion drew me in, and ultimately, over many months, the study changed my heart, pulling me out of a metaphorical pit.

Carla started studying to be a life coach. She needed hours of practice sessions to finish her certification. She asked me to do her the favor of allowing her to coach me for free. I told her she must really want the hours if she is asking me to do this. I warned her that I was still carrying so much bottled-up negativity. Sweet Carla and her little dog sat and listened without judgment for hours as I cried, got angry, unleashed my bitterness, and said many words that are not in the Bible. Most of all, Carla helped me to feel heard and find healing. I sincerely believe that without Carla, I wouldn't have taken the next steps into a new season that included launching and hosting a podcast. And I wouldn't be writing this book right now. God used her in a powerful way.

My faith grew as I continued to attend the Bible study group and developed a love for God and His Word. One day I reflected on some of the miraculous ways God moved through my injury and in the months to follow. I fell to my knees in tears realizing I am only living because He saved me. For the first time, I completely surrendered my whole life to Jesus. I remember these words flowing from my mouth, "Whatever you want me to do, God, I will do it. I want to live for You. I want to use the rest of my days to serve You because You are my everything." After much healing, I was divinely led to launch the podcast in 2018, which officially reached over 1 million downloads recently. I can hardly believe it!

In retrospect, I see how staying isolated kept me locked up and bitter. All those harmful emotions festered in my heart. I had no joy or peace. I am so grateful that God used Carla to help me get unstuck. I had no idea how much I needed those women. It felt so amazing to have a group I could confide in, confess things to, pray with, praise with, study with, and serve alongside.

Jesus does not want us isolated. He is all about community. The Scriptures tell us to bear one another's burdens, encourage and help one another. When recording testimonies and hearing some of my podcast guests share their darkest, often tragic moments, they frequently share that they felt God's all-consuming love through the prayers, service, and presence of other believers. That all-consuming love comforts and strengthens us to keep serving God and people.

What Does the Science Say About Isolation?

The Amen Clinic shared an article entitled, "What Social Isolation is Really Doing to Your Health," dated July 30, 2020, which included in summary 7 TROUBLING CONSEQUENCES OF LONELINESS:

1. Increased risk of Alzheimer's disease and other dementias by 40%.

2. Cognitive decline in ages 65 and over increased by 20%.

3. Psychiatric disorders, including depression, substance use disorders, sleep problems, and personality disorders.

4. Heightened risk of suicide and increased risk of drug addiction.

5. Altered brain development with marked overall decreased activity across the whole brain.

6. Physical health risks equal to smoking 15 cigarettes a day or having an alcohol use disorder. Social isolation and loneliness have twice the harmful effects of obesity.

7. Impaired immune system.[10]

Isolation is no joke! Did you catch the last sentence in point six? Isolation is two times as harmful as obesity! Two times! WOW! I think I will phone a friend right now.

Dreadlocks are for Toddlers Too

We woke the kids early, maybe 4-5 a.m., to make the flight to Orlando. Kendal was two and a half, Anders was four, and we were heading to Florida to fulfill a bucket list item to take a vacation at a theme park. As usual, I was a bit stressed with all the packing, getting to the airport, and dealing with precious yet exhausted children. Kendal has always had sensory issues, and it had been a fight to brush her hair for years. She wouldn't let me touch her hair that day, and I didn't have the energy or time to battle over it.

We finally made it to the airplane, and I already felt worn out and a little guilty before the start of our magical adventure. A woman boarded with her children in tow, arms full and looking just as haggard as me. I could feel that her stress matched mine. As she waited near my aisle, I looked up at her and said, "Hey, look at mine over here; she's sporting dreadlocks." She laughed when she saw my daughter's crazy hair. I continued, "But you know what? We won (referring to us moms). We made it onto the airplane. That was really all we had to do this morning, and we did it." We high-fived and laughed, and instantly, all the stress completely dissipated. We had a moment. I can't speak for her, but my whole day shifted out of stress mode.

Women Need Other Women

I love my husband wholeheartedly, but sometimes I just need a trusted female friend I can relate to, confide in, laugh with, and connect one-on-one. Generally speaking, women are more nurturing, empathic, and expressive. Great Biblical examples of these special bonds are Mary and her cousin Elizabeth, and Ruth and Naomi. In the example of Ruth's words to Naomi (Ruth 1:16-17), *"But Ruth replied, 'Don't urge me to leave you or to turn back from you. Where you go, I will go, and where you stay I will stay. Your people will be my people and your God my God. Where you die, I will die, and there I will be buried. May the LORD deal with me, be it ever so severely if even death separates you and me.'"* (NIV)

The old expression, "it takes a village," was originally meant to express that it takes more than one set of parents to raise a child. But I think I now believe that it is also about caring for the family as a unit. God uses everyone, whether family or not, to help and encourage us. We are in this together. We need each other.

Reflect

Have you ever fallen into the trap of isolation? _____

What can you do today to find a healthy community where you can grow?

_____

_____

_____

_____

_____

_____

Do you have a church home that is helping you to grow spiritually? _____

When was the last time you reached out to be a friend to someone in need?

_____

_____

_____

_____

_____

_____

_____

What the Bible says about friendship and community:

- John 15:12-13, "This is my commandment: Love each other in the same way I have loved you. There is no greater love than to lay down one's life for one's friends" (NLT).

- Psalms 133:1, "How wonderful and pleasant it is when brothers live together in harmony!" (NLT).

- 1 Thessalonians 5:11, "So encourage each other and build each other up, just you are already doing" (NLT).

- Colossians 3:13-14, "Make allowances for each other's faults and forgive anyone who offends you. Remember the Lord forgave you, so you must forgive others. Above all, clothe yourselves with love, which binds us all together in perfect harmony" (NLT).

- Galatians 6:2, "Share each other's burdens, and in this way obey the law of Christ" (NLT).

- Galatians 6:10, "Therefore, whenever we have the opportunity, we should do good to everyone – especially to those in the family of faith" (NLT).

- Hebrews 10:24-25, "Let us think of ways to motivate one another to acts of love and good works. And let us not neglect our meeting together, as some people do, but encourage one another, especially now that the day of his return is drawing near" (NLT).

- Romans 12:4-5, "Just as our bodies have many parts and each part has a special function, so it is with Christ's body. We are many parts of one body, and we all belong to each other" (NLT).

Some Scriptures for those feeling isolated:

- James 4:8, "Come close to God, and God will come close to you" (NLT).

- Deuteronomy 31:8, "Do not be afraid or discouraged, for the Lord will personally go ahead of you. He will be with you; he will neither fail you nor abandon you" (NLT).

- Psalms 147:3, "He heals the brokenhearted and bandages their wounds" (NLT).

- Matthew 28:20, "Teach these new disciples to obey all the commands I have given you. And be sure of this: I am with you always, even to the end of the age" (NLT).

- Isaiah 41:10, "Don't be afraid, for I am with you. Don't be discouraged, for I am your God. I will strengthen you and help you. I will hold you up with my victorious right hand" (NLT).

PRAYER FOR THOSE TEMPTED TO ISOLATE

Dear heavenly Father,

Thank You that You promise never to leave us!
Thank You, Lord, that You see me and hear my prayers.
Please come and fill my heart with Your presence.
Strengthen me to reach out and lead me to a group of
women where I can find connection, fellowship, and mutual
support. Help me to be a blessing to others and to know
the joy of belonging again.

In Jesus' name, amen!

"An empty tank will take you exactly nowhere. Take time to refuel."
— Anonymous

Pitfall #5 – NEGLECTING SELF-CARE

Spirit. Mind. and Body

A young mother checked her baby (or babies) into the gym nursery at Lifetime Fitness and was seen sleeping in the front gym lobby. I didn't see her, but I heard about her and had mixed emotions. My first thought was admiration because she found a way to get desperately needed rest. She was taking care of herself. My second thought was sadness because she needed help and may not have the support of her family or community. As I write this section, I can't help but think of single moms and those without the financial resources to get the help they need. I don't have all the answers, but I pray that some of the tools I share in this book can equip and empower you.

Selflessness and Self-Care

Selflessness is a beautiful thing. Jesus Christ himself was a perfect example of selflessness. We are told in Scripture to love one another. We have the famous parable of the selflessness of the Good Samaritan and the historical reference of Esther willingly risking her life to help the Jews. In the Book of Philippians (2:3-4), Paul writes, *"Instead of being motivated by selfish ambition or vanity, each of you should, in humility, be moved to treat one another as more important than yourself. Each of you should be concerned not only about your own interests, but about the interests of others as well."*

You and I need to understand that it is selfless to take care of yourself. Remember, it's for others as much as it is for you, so take time for yourSELF.

Jesus Took Naps

Personally, I have found the balance between selflessness and self-care to be complicated. We are instructed to care for our temple (body) and to guard our hearts and minds. We are told not to throw our pearls to swine (Matthew 7:6). We know that even Jesus had times when he had to retreat to the garden to rest and pray (Matthew 6 and 14). In the Book of Mark, He took a nap on the boat as a storm developed. Now, remember, Jesus was fully God and fully man (Titus 2:13-14). He had three short years to spread his message, perform miracles, and fulfill His mission on Earth, and He took breaks when He needed them.

Mothers carry many responsibilities and needs for self, spouse, children, family, friends, schools, aging parents, church-family, charity, and ministry. How do we serve selflessly and not get lost in the process? Sure, we need to set healthy boundaries, but with finite time and resources, it can be difficult to determine what comes first. Does setting healthy boundaries always include something else being sacrificed? I don't know if this is something anyone truly masters, but we must set priorities and find our way to manage them daily to the best of our ability. We must know where to draw the line when things get out of balance.

SELF-CARE INCLUDES CARING FOR YOUR SPIRIT

Spiritual Care

"I was looking down on my body from the ceiling, (pointing) right there."

Did you know that hospitals have special departments dedicated solely to providing spiritual care? Yes, a whole group of amazing Chaplains serve in hospitals to help care for people spiritually in a place where people are suffering acutely with the physical. We are truly a spirit first. I have personally witnessed evidence of this while working as a nurse in the Cardiovascular Intensive Care Unit. A patient clinically dies, is unresponsive, blue, and pulseless for 4-6 minutes. He is resuscitated and can tell me, with complete accuracy, everything that happened in the room as he watched as he was "floating near the ceiling." So, how do we care for our spirit? What does that look like in real-time?

Jesus retreated to quiet places to pray so he could be strengthened by spending time with his Father. Matthew 6:33 (NLT) states very clearly, *"Seek the Kingdom of God above all else, and live righteously, and he will give you everything you need."* We strengthen our spirits when we pray, when we are still to hear from God, and when we read His word. Worshipping alone or corporately is another way to connect spiritually with God. I often see God in the beauty of nature and His creation around me in a beautiful rainbow, a flower, a sunset, a majestic horse, and even the smallest butterfly.

Surrendering my life fully and completely to God and asking to receive the Holy Spirit was pivotal in my spiritual life. Although I grew up as a Christian, I did not fully surrender my life to God, as I shared earlier, until after my neck injury in 2015. It is so true that when you seek Him with all your heart, you will find Him. As a result of my surrender, I have a new relationship with Jesus that changes everything. I know He is with me, and I feel that spiritual connection. I seek His counsel on things, and I am learning to hear His voice more and more. I can't imagine life without Him.

Prayer is Critical for Our Self-Care

Prayer is selfless, self-care. How is your prayer life? God wants us to be still and listen, and He wants us to pray without ceasing (1 Thess. 5:17). He tells us to present our requests to him. Prayer is how we connect to God. It is simply a conversation with God. He wants an intimate relationship with us, and prayer is a big part of our connection to Him. One of the fun things about hearing testimonies is all the many ways people hear from God. Do you realize God is speaking to you?

"My sheep listen to my voice; I know them, and they follow me" John 10:27 (NLT). *For God speaks again and again, though people do not recognize it. He speaks in dreams, in visions of the night, when deep sleep falls on people as they lie in their beds"* Job 33:14 (NLT).

"Your own ears will hear him. Right behind you a voice will say, "This is the way you should go," whether to the right or to the left" Isaiah 30:21 (NLT)

Is that You God or Grocery Store Sushi?

I have one friend who hears God so clearly that she can ask Him what to put in her coffee and get a response (and she is in her Bible more than anyone I know). I don't hear Him that succinctly. The first time I knew I heard God speak to me, I thought maybe I had eaten something bad. I didn't even know it was Him! I had a thought that came into my head while I was at work.

I intubated a patient after a smooth induction of anesthesia. As I turned to put my laryngoscope away, I heard, "This part of your life is over." It was so clear in my head I felt it could have been audible. The tone gave a gentle and calm authority but with matter-of-fact conviction. My heart sank to the floor. I can still see the scene in my mind when I heard it. Confused and sad, I went home to tell Lars and asked him a few times, "Why would I think that? I don't understand why I would think that!" I actually wondered if I had eaten some old grocery store sushi.

My injury happened sometime after I received this message. It wasn't until a few years later and seeing where God has taken me, that I realized God was preparing me, letting me know it was time to leave my job (which I fought to keep for some time). I was slow on the uptake, but God has limitless grace and was patient with me. Prayer and hearing from God are essential to our spiritual health, which is part of self-care.

How Does God Speak to People?

God speaks to us clearly through reading His Word, which is the surest way to hear from God. How do all these people I have interviewed hear from God? One of my podcast episodes was about this exact topic. Jill Monaco of Jill Monaco Ministries shared that there are typically four general categories. However, we aren't limited to one, and they can change over time as God is developing us. *Hearing* (audible or in thought), *seeing* (dreams or visions), *feeling* (an internal impression or gut instinct), and *knowing* (a strong belief or conviction) are the four general ways she shares that people often hear from God on a day-to-day basis[11].

Guests on my show share how they have heard from God in more ways than I can count. There have been guests who see angels, have dreams and visions, or see the love of Jesus in the eyes of their compassionate nurse. Some say they heard a clear message from God through a song, through repeated patterns of numbers, messages from other people that keep reverberating, and in a pair of perfectly timed Batman socks that had a strong sentimental value. Another is through a literal sign, in a prophetic message from a stranger at Target, a man's dentist sharing that God put a message on his heart that he had to share, and so many more.

One guest heard from God when a boy reeled in a fish, and the fish looked at her and spoke in plain English, only to her, that the boy would be her husband. I had no idea she would share that, and I confess I immediately heard the Billy Bass song in my head, "Take me to the river, drop me in the water." Thank goodness I kept focused. Remember God spoke through a donkey in the Bible, and he sent a coin through a fish's mouth. It is Biblical that He speaks and works through animals. My guest married that young fisherman, and they have enjoyed a long life together, last I heard. God speaks to people in countless different ways!

I am especially blown away at the number of people who have heard God's audible voice. Several of my guests experienced God's audible voice. Chaplain David Carl did when he received his calling from God; others at low points in their lives or in life-threatening circumstances. I can't say I have ever heard God audibly, but I feel strong, sometimes sudden, internal impressions. I now recognize God is leading me, as these moments have proven, in many cases, to be confirmed. Many times, someone will pop into my head, and I will feel led to pray. I will send a text prayer, only to get a message back, "How did you know I am in the emergency room?" Next time someone pops into your head, it may be God prompting you to pray for them. Ask Him to lead you.

I am not an expert on this, but I can tell you that God will speak to you. If you don't feel you are hearing Him, I suggest praying and asking God to help you in this area. Get into the Bible and read so you know His character, which helps you to know Him and hear Him clearly. He will not contradict the Bible. I often pray and ask God to speak to my spirit in my dreams at night. I also ask Him to make His messages plain and simple and help me to see/hear/feel it (and He does!). The hardest part? For me, the hardest part is being still and listening! For me, it is not on-demand communication. Sometimes when I am desperately asking, I hear nothing, and other times that seem random, I hear a message so clearly. Perhaps we are being tested, or God is doing a work in us! He may even be trying to draw us nearer to Him through silence.

Another fascinating thing I have noticed in hearing so many different testimonies is the frequency of people with near-death testimonies who realize the power of prayer in heaven. These are subjective reports, and we need always to use discernment and go with the Word of God first, but I find it so interesting to hear these guests talk about seeing prayers coming to heaven from Earth. Jim Woodford saw prayers shooting up and described them as streaks of brilliant light going straight up, painting the heavenly sky[12].

Another testimony I heard in an interview by fellow podcaster, Shaun Tabatt, described the power of people praying scriptural prayers and how they would rise upwards to form vertical bridges up to heaven[13]. One man said when he nearly died while in a coma that he saw heaven in the distance, but as he was trying to move towards it, the prayers were like a wind that was pushing him back into his body. After doing over a year of near-death testimony interviews, Shaun Tabatt shares that one thing that impressed him greatly is the power of a mother's prayer. He shares that people have reported they have been snatched from the gates of hell and given a second chance because of a mother's prayer[14]. He jokes that dads need to step up their prayer game. Bottom line, our prayers have power!

An Essential Note about Near-Death Testimonies and Spirituality

If you are a new believer, I desperately want you to understand that there is absolutely a spiritual realm, and there are things we can unknowingly do to put ourselves in spiritual danger. Some Christians choose to reject all near-death and supernatural testimonies. I understand and respect this viewpoint. Leading you into the land of near-death testimonies without a solid Biblical foundation would throw you onto a field laced with land mines and put you at significant risk. Scripture tells you where those land mines are located (figuratively).

We have an enemy out to steal, kill, and destroy[15]. He loves to confuse and trick us. The Bible is clear that he can appear as a "being of light[16]." We are also warned about the dangers of mediums, tarot cards, and the new age. All testimonies are subjective, and we must always compare how they line up with scripture and use discernment given by the Holy Spirit. The Bible is always the framework for our theology. If you are new to faith, the first and only place to start your study is with God's Word. Many say the King James Version is the best but find one you can read and understand, then start there.

So why have I shared near-death testimonies and included some of their characteristics in this spiritual section? I have felt led by God to share some of these testimonies. I absolutely believe those I have shared. One was an adamant atheist, another a Jewish woman who was told her whole life that Jesus was a hoax, as well as others coming back and testifying that they had similar near-death experiences. Many of them heard Scripture in their encounter, giving them a new hunger for and understanding of the Bible. Those get my attention. I believe God is doing something through these experiences. Hearing so many testimonies with the same message, "Tell them what you saw, tell them I am coming soon, tell them they are loved more than they could imagine," is compelling.

Why do so many believers reject near-death testimonies? I think they can become idols. We need to be in the Word more than binging these testimonies. Also, as I implied above, the enemy can use them to draw us into something dangerous and demonic. Some have been found to be false accounts. Some people may be creating their experiences to get attention. I do think it is natural for us to be curious and drawn to these supernatural things because, at our core, we are spiritual beings, but we need to be careful.

Our culture is fascinated with angels, horror movies, ghosts, and the paranormal. Although hell is Biblical (Matthew 13:42, Matthew 25:41), many Christians do not believe in it[17] (21% according to Pew Research Center, 2021). We seem to pick and choose what is acceptable and whacky in our culture. I find it comical when I see friends at church or school who run up with wide eyes and whisper, "I heard your episode about the person who saw heaven!" Is it something dirty that they don't want to be overheard? It makes me laugh. Why the weirdness? Maybe God is sending a message to us, as Pastor and Author John Burke proposes, "Coloring in the picture of what God has been revealing through Scripture all along[18]."

It intrigues me when people come back and share how they can understand the Bible like never before. My Jewish friend was criticized by some in her community for sharing that she met Jesus. She was so taken with Him that she moved to Israel and lived for a year to soak in everything she could. She learned Hebrew and studied His life. So many that potentially suffer for sharing, whether professionally or otherwise, have come forward with these reports. Some experiencers return, expressing things straight from the Bible that they didn't know were in Scripture. Blind people have these experiences and have sight when out of their bodies[19]. One woman saw things in her life review that were later proven accurate, with no way she could have known what she shared (see John Burke's book entitled, *Imagine Heaven*).

God has confirmed His leading for me to share NDEs through the feedback I have gotten from listeners. One woman's husband works for a large popular Christian ministry. She wrote me and confessed her faith had stalled and that listening to the testimonies had stirred her faith up again. Another young lady said that listening to Charlotte Holmes' near-death testimony led her to read the entire Bible for the first time in her life. She developed a relationship with Jesus that she had never known was possible. Through these testimonies, I always point people to Jesus and His Word. I diligently pray that they are used according to His will. Everyone will not agree with me, and it is ok.

SELF-CARE INCLUDES OUR THOUGHT LIFE

The Battle for Our Thoughts is Real

Did you realize that our minds are a battleground for spiritual warfare? It sounds very dramatic, but our thoughts can be from the enemy, self, or God. The Bible speaks about taking every thought captive[20] for this reason. Learning to distinguish these thoughts or voices is critical. Here is a simple list of how to discern the source:

Enemy's voice/message	God's voice/message
worries you	comforts you
shames, condemns, guilts you	convicts you
confuses you	enlightens you
obsesses or rushes you	calms or stills you
pressures or pushes you	guides or leads you
belittles or discourages you	encourages or inspires you
frightens you	reassures you

It takes practice, but when the thoughts in the left column creep in, stop and recognize, resist, pray, and ask God to show you the truth. If there is a particular issue that keeps popping up for you, find a Bible verse that speaks against it and keep it on your phone (or in your pocket if you are doing a digital detox) and claim the fullness of the verse when those thoughts pop up again.

"Finally, brothers, whatever is true, whatever is noble, whatever is right, whatever is pure, whatever is lovely, whatever is admirable—if anything is excellent or praiseworthy—think about these things" Philippians 4:8 (NIV).

SELF-CARE INCLUDES OUR MIND

Mental Health

"Don't copy the behavior and customs of this world, but let God transform you into a new person by changing the way you think. Then you will learn to know God's will for you, which is good and pleasing and perfect," Romans 12:2 (NLT).

I still remember the grocery store check-out tabloid with Kelly Clarkson's shocked face with a headline something to the effect of, "Kelly Clarkson sends her kids to therapy in midst of a nasty divorce." I was so mad at how the tabloid seemed to portray therapy as something shameful! Congratulations, Kelly, for being a responsible parent and taking a proactive role in the mental health of your children. I wish my parents had the money to send me to therapy when they divorced.

Why do we still have such a stigma with therapy in our culture? Therapy is good for everyone! Therapy promotes mental health and provides coping skills. We should be applauding those that are seeking to improve their mental health. I remember someone talking about their therapist openly in a Bible study, which was so refreshing. We should embrace these efforts to heal and grow.

My Psych Rotation

I hated my psych rotation in nursing school. There, I said it. We were taught how to use therapeutic communication (there were some words you couldn't say), which I found stifling. When a patient became combative during a psychotic episode, we were trained on how to do takedowns and use physical force to restrain people to keep them and others safe. I hated takedowns. I didn't know how to help these poor people. I couldn't see their issue on an x-ray or fix it with a splint. Medication only seemed to sedate them, not fix their issue.

Although there were many patients I quickly connected with and hopefully helped, overall, there was a lot of heartache in my empathic chest. As a Nurse Anesthetist, I have done anesthesia for hundreds of electro-convulsive shock therapy treatments on patients. While they were always asleep for the shocks to their brains, it felt so barbaric to me. I will say that many of those patients did see improvement, and there was joy when I would see them again, no longer catatonic but holding eye contact, almost a smile developing. I have so much respect for those led to this area of nursing and medicine. It is a calling, and it is needed. If that's you, thank you for your work.

Fortunately, since the '90s, there have been so many advances in mental health and new, less invasive treatments available to help people overcome traumas and cope with different mental/emotional disorders. We all have the same neurotransmitters, but not everyone's brain is balanced or created equally. I am all for natural and conservative approaches, but I have seen the extreme, and I believe sometimes medical intervention is necessary.

Seeing these extremes, I never thought of myself needing psychiatric care, but there have been some revelations in the past several years. Let me share.

Violent Flock of Seagulls on the Beach

There was a discount on a second brain scan at the Amen Clinic. I was there with a loved one and decided to take advantage of this luxury to look at my brain health. I did the first set of scans (after doing lots of concentration exercises), and the next day I arrived to do the scan at rest. A classic overachiever, I imagined I was relaxing on a beautiful beach, zoned out, and looked forward to how great my results would be in my peaceful state.

Shockingly, there was an attack of seagulls on that beach because my results were not what I expected. I knew I had issues with anxiety, but I didn't expect the Post Traumatic Stress Disorder and some other things that would show up. I think I had existed in such an anxious state for so long that it became my normal. I was just powering through life and not addressing some needed issues with my mental health. I am still battling with anxiety, but I am making progress.

While not everyone can spend money on a brain scan, we can all take a moment to evaluate our mental health and what routines are we putting in place to care for our brains. Are we so anxious that we don't rest at night? Are we able to settle our minds? Are we meditating and doing deep breathing exercises? Are there traumas we have buried that need to be addressed? Are we holding unforgiveness, repressed emotions, bitterness, or other negative emotions? Are we recognizing unhealthy triggers that are contributing to other behaviors that aren't serving us?

Support for Mental Wellness is Available

If you have the resources to pursue testing or therapy, great! If not, there are many free or economical ways to find help. If you have a specific area of struggle, there are support groups for almost everything. I found one for vertebral artery dissection patients, which is reportedly rare. Churches have them for many different groups. There are groups for overeaters, groups for moms of special needs kids, groups for divorce support, and the list goes on. It may feel scary to go the first time, and you may have to try a few different groups to find your people, but they are out there.

Some Christians don't utilize therapists and assert that God can heal everything. Well, I agree that God can heal everything. I also believe that God also works through people. I found a

Christian therapist who has a seminary degree and practices the same faith, and I think God has equipped her with specific gifts. She has been a huge blessing to me and helped me to find healing and new ways to cope with struggles.

There are also tons of applications now to help you with gratitude practice (I love 5-Minute Journal), mindfulness and meditation. There is a Neurocycle app created by Dr. Caroline Leaf that enables you to rewire and detox the brain. There are new treatment modalities as well that don't include medication. One that I have tried and enjoyed is called neurofeedback (although this is not available in all cities). Therapists can do EMDR (eye movement desensitization and reprocessing), alpha-stim electrotherapy, brain spotting, and other processes in sessions that have proven successful for many patients. Thank you, God, for neuroplasticity (our brains can change and heal in more ways than we may realize)!

Therapy costs money. If you cannot afford it, there are still so many free and powerful ways to find help. There are free programs and apps for your phone to help you with meditation. I like Abide. Even doing simple deep breathing exercises can have an immediate calming effect on your nervous system. A few apps recommended by the American Institute of Stress: Calm, PTSD Coach, Headspace, Tactical Breather, and Serenita.

SELF-CARE INCLUDES THE PHYSICAL BODY

Physical Health

When I interview empty nest moms, physical health is one of the most common things they say they wish they had done differently. Many wish they had taken better care of their physical bodies. I am not a doctor, but as a former nurse who is married to a man who does high-level coaching, I have attended nearly every type of personal development course you can imagine in the last ten years. They all include teaching about the importance of physical health.

No, I have not yet mastered this area, but I have made lots of progress and am equipped and hopeful that I will find my optimal state of physical health. Physical health looks different for everyone, based on your body type and health condition. I have severe scoliosis and a history of vertebral artery dissections, so I have found what works for me and my structure. Partnering with the proper health care professional is always a good idea when implementing a new fitness or dietary regimen.

Most of us know what to do to live a healthy lifestyle: more whole foods, more clean foods, moving our bodies, getting enough sleep, hydration, avoiding toxins, and managing stress levels. I remember Tony Robbins on the stage, emphatically stating, *"Unmanaged stress is worse than a bad diet."* Of course, he is all about eating clean as well, and he drinks no alcohol.

There are many diets and fitness options, including free workout videos and meal prep ideas online. Find what works for you and make it a priority (Sister, I am working on this too.).

Get your labs checked as you can and supplement as you need. I am a big fan of functional medicine, although the physician I am seeing now is an MD that also incorporates functional medicine. These are costly, but if you can get basic lab work and identify a problem before it spirals out of control, it costs much less in the long run than a health crisis. Being intentional and consistent with caring for our physical body will decrease the risk of disease and add both years and quality to our lives.

SELF-CARE INCLUDES SELF-TALK

Speak Life

Words matter. Do you have a habit of being critical as you speak about yourself? These could be big statements or small subtle jabs, but they have power in your mind. I saw the validity of this when working as a nurse. Your brain is listening. And the Word of God says, "As a man thinks in his heart, so is he." Your thoughts become words, and your words produce either life or death. Here's how it impacted me years ago.

I was a brand-new nurse in the Cardiovascular Intensive Care Unit. I was eager to be thorough, so I asked my open-heart patients all the questions on my chart so my little perfectionist nurse heart could check them off diligently. "Do you have nausea?" was one of the questions on the list. I made sure they were comfortable and reviewed with them plans for the night, making sure the call light was within reach. Almost inevitably, within 15-30 minutes, they were throwing up, and I was running to the pyxis machine for rescue antiemetics. It seemed my patients were always puking those few first nights while most of the others in the unit were resting.

The next shift, I had an idea. I didn't ask the list of questions. I simply shared observations and emphasized all the things that were positive or just normal. "Your blood pressure looks great! Your urine output is fantastic. I checked your labs, and they were excellent. You are doing so well!" Their faces would light up. After this, I simply asked one open-ended question, "How are you feeling?" Miraculously, my patients' rates of post-op nausea dropped dramatically. I didn't record the statistics, and of course, it was not absolute, but I realized by asking about nausea, I was planting a seed in their minds that they should be nauseated. There is a way to provide excellent care that also benefits the patient's mindset. The same applies to your self-care. Speak words of life over yourself and reap the benefits. Our words have power!

Daily Affirmations

Many years ago, Stuart Smalley played a Saturday Night Live skit character where the host looked at himself in a mirror and practiced daily affirmations. The skit premise required the host to be riddled with insecurities and a member of multiple 12 Step programs without training.

I admit it was funny, but I think it minimized the simple process and power of speaking affirmations over yourself.

Is There Science to Support the Power of Daily Affirmations?

There is neuroscience to prove that this simple practice is effective:

"A study published in the journal *Social Cognitive and Affective Neuroscience* revealed what goes on in our brains when we practice affirmations regularly. The researchers used MRI to find that practicing self-affirmation activates the reward centers–ventral striatum (VS) and ventromedial prefrontal cortex (VMPFC) in the brain. Simply put, these areas are the same reward centers that respond to other pleasurable experiences, such as eating your favorite dish or winning a prize." The lead researcher, Christopher Cascio said, 'Many studies have shown that these circuits can do things like dampen pain and help us maintain balance in the face of threats.' Thus practicing self-affirmation does help in activating those areas of the brain that makes you happy and positive[21]."

From another article, "Benefits of Daily Affirmations": Now that we know more about the theories supporting positive affirmations, here are six examples of evidence from empirical studies that suggest that positive self-affirmation practices can be beneficial:

1. Self-affirmations have been shown to decrease health-deteriorating stress.

2. Self-affirmations have been used effectively in interventions that led people to increase their physical behavior.

3. They may help us to perceive otherwise "threatening" messages with less resistance, including interventions.

4. They can make us less likely to dismiss harmful health messages, responding instead with the intention to change for the better and to eat more fruit and vegetables.

5. They have been linked positively to academic achievement by mitigating GPA decline in students who feel left out at college.

6. Self-affirmation has been demonstrated to lower stress and rumination.[22]

Wow! Visible changes noted on MRI and evidence from empirical studies point to the potential for affirmations!

Ask someone close to you to share their opinion on how you speak over yourself.

Reflect

How are you caring for yourself: spirit, mind, and body?

_____

_____

Which areas are you managing well, and which areas can you improve?

_____

_____

What is one simple thing you can do today to improve one of these areas?

_____

_____

How is your prayer life? Can you find a time daily to be still to hear from God?

_____

_____

How is your thought life? Do you recognize any thoughts that are not from God? How will you address it next time it pops into your head?

_____

_____

How would you evaluate your self-talk?

_____

_____

What does the Bible say about the words we speak?

- Proverbs 18:21, "The tongue can bring death or life; those who love to talk will reap the consequences" (NLT).

- Ephesians 4:29, "Don't use foul or abusive language. Let everything you say be good and helpful, so that your words will be an encouragement to those who hear them" (NLT).

- Proverbs 15:4, "Gentle words are a tree of life; a deceitful tongue crushes the spirit" (NLT).

- Proverbs 13:3, "Those who control their tongue will have a long life; opening your mouth can ruin everything" (NLT).

What does the Bible say about self-care?

- Ephesians 5:29, "No one hates his own body but feeds and cares for it, just as Christ cares for the church" (NLT).

- 1 Corinthians 6:19-20, "Don't you realize that your body is the temple of the Holy Spirit, who lives in you and was given to you by God? You do not belong to yourself, for God bought you with a high price. So you must honor God with your body" (NLT).

- Luke 5:16, "But Jesus often withdrew to the wilderness for prayer" (NLT).

- Proverbs 4:23, "Guard your heart above all else, for it determines the course of your life" (NLT).

PRAYER FOR MOMS IN THE AREA OF SELF-CARE

Dear heavenly Father,

Thank You for creating our amazing bodies, minds, and spirits.
Thank You for Your Word that offers wisdom on how to care
for ourselves. Please forgive me when I get caught up in "busy
mode" and try to do everything in my power. Help me set
healthy boundaries and rely on You. Revitalize my spirit and
give my body and mind needed rest.

I thank You in advance for your energy and strength that will
sustain me.

In Jesus' name, amen!

PULLING IT ALL TOGETHER

Your Breakthrough is Here!

SUMMARY FOR BUSY MOMS

Steps To Triumph Over My Common Pitfalls.

#1 Comparison

Become more self-aware of triggers and avoid them. If you are on social media, consider a digital detox or set time limits, remove what is triggering you and add what fuels you! Count your blessings and remember what makes you unique. Celebrate with others when they have victories and be an encourager! Meditate on the Scriptures provided for this pitfall.

#2 Perfectionism

Get perspective on unrealistic expectations and the cost they carry. Work on mindfulness, being present, and looking for things to appreciate in the moment. Practice gratitude by journaling or add a quick gratitude app on your phone that you can do quickly in the morning and night to get your mind in a healthy place. Know when to seek professional help if needed.

#3 Fear

Trust God. Pray. Get into the Bible and meditate on the Scriptures that are specific to your fears. Build your faith by listening to testimonies, inspiring sermons, or podcasts. *Equip & Empower* with Christine Caine podcast is like spiritual caffeine. Be aware of things that are triggering fear that can be removed (e.g., too much news). Enjoy things that soothe your soul, whatever that is for you (music, nature, animals). The Pour Over is a Christian podcast and email news provider that just lists the news facts without bias and offers Scriptures to pray over current events. Check out free applications for anxiety, meditation, gratitude, and deep breathing.

#4 Isolation

Find your people! We are wired for human connection. Women need other women. It is more evident now than ever that isolation has serious effects on health and wellness. Find an inner circle that you can trust, where you can support and pray for one another, one that accepts you for the real you. If you have a unique situation, find people that you can relate to for added support in that specific area (e.g., addiction, special needs child, divorce support, etc.). Churches have small groups. Communities have health centers and social events, clubs, and charity events where you can get involved and even be a blessing to others!

#5 Neglect of Self-care

Start with an honest assessment of your spiritual, mental, and physical health and decide where you need to focus first. Set some goals for your prayer life, moving your body, nutrition, sleep, and hydration. You can start with one goal and gradually add if it feels overwhelming. You will model great habits for your kids, and they will see you excel! Read the affirmations or find the free online video and listen to them. Set healthy boundaries. If it feels heavy to say yes, then say no. If it's not something that you really want to do, that may be your discernment. Honor yourself and say no when necessary.

I have been blessed to meet many moms around the world and even care for people from many cultures as a nurse. As a result, I've learned:

1. We are not so different.
2. None of us have it all together.
3. First and foremost, we need Jesus so we have access to God.
4. We need each other.
5. We need grace.
6. We need love and care for ourselves.
7. We need joy and peace.
8. We long to feel heard, understood, connected, and accepted.

What's been my prayer as I have written this book? Breakthrough! It is time for your breakthrough, and mine too. It is time to remember who we were created to be and to recognize and put into practice the dynamite, supernatural power of our prayers. Let's embrace our uniqueness as we reconnect and let God lead us into the Divine plan He created for us!

AFFIRMATIONS & DECLARATIONS FOR MOMS

Here are some that I have found helpful for moms who anchor their identity in Jesus:

Because the Holy Spirit dwells in me, I possess all His fruit:

I am filled with God's love

I am filled with the joy of the Lord

I have perfect peace in chaos

I have infinite patience

I am kind

I am filled with God's goodness, and my actions reflect this

I am faithful to God and others

I have self-control, and I stay disciplined in ways that Honor God

I take care of my body, mind, and spirit

Because I am His child:

I am chosen by God

I am beautiful

I have a spirit of power, love, and self-control

I am enough

I matter

I am cared for

I am lovable and deeply loved

I am content in all situations

I see and appreciate the good all around me

I am healed by His stripes

I am worthy

I am capable

I am seen

I am strong in the Lord

I am full of hope, and it radiates from me as I enter a room

I am victorious

I am resourceful

I am an overcomer

I am God's masterpiece

I have a purpose and plan determined by God

I am forgiven

I am redeemed

I am anointed

I am fearfully and wonderfully made

My name is written on God's hand

Jesus died for ME

In Christ Jesus, I possess all that I need

God has entrusted these children to me

God is equipping me

Jesus is making a place for me in heaven

I trust the Lord, and he guides my steps

God is teaching me and leading me

I am blessed and highly favored

I am present

I see and appreciate His beautiful creation all around me

I am filled with gratitude

I have unlimited potential because I can do all things through Christ

I trust God to do the impossible

I am protected

I trust God when I am afraid

God's power can work in my weakness

I surrender my burdens to Jesus

I am courageous; the Lord is my stronghold

I am free

I am never alone

I am free of condemnation

I am a child of God

I am a citizen of Heaven

I receive the rest and comfort God gives me

I have perfect peace because I trust in God

I trust God's timing

I declare that no weapon formed against me will prosper

I allow nothing to sabotage my identity in Christ and the plans He has for me

Nothing can separate me from the love of God

My hope is the Lord, and I will wait on Him and trust Him for my life and future

Maybe you would like to write some affirmations for yourself:

1. _____
2. _____
3. _____
4. _____
5. _____
6. _____
7. _____
8. _____
9. _____
10. _____
11. _____
12. _____
13. _____
14. _____
15. _____

IF YOU HAVE NEVER ACCEPTED JESUS CHRIST

We now have more evidence for Jesus Christ than ever[23](Imagine Heaven appendix reference). Biblical prophecies are being fulfilled, and the pages of Revelation are coming alive[24]. There is a fault line in the Earth exactly where the Bible says it will split at the Mount of Olives on the day Jesus returns[25] (Zechariah14:4). Reports of meeting Jesus in dreams, visions, and near-death experiences are happening in unprecedented numbers for atheists, agnostics, and others far from Christ. Many of these people are sharing that Jesus told them to share what they have seen and that He is coming soon.

The definition of faith found in Hebrews states, "the assurance of things hoped for, the conviction of things not seen" (Hebrews 11:1). If you have never accepted Jesus, and you want to take that step, it is easy, and it will absolutely change your life and your eternity.

All you need is an open and sincere heart. You are already loved more than you can imagine, and Jesus is here and waiting for your invitation. All you have to say is, "Dear Jesus, I believe that you are the Son of God, that you died for me so that I could be forgiven of my sins. I want to surrender my life to you. Please forgive me and come into my life to be my personal Lord and Savior. Thank you, Jesus, for saving me! In your precious name, amen!" If you just prayed that prayer, heaven is rejoicing over you! Congrats on the most important decision you can make in this life!

ONE LAST SWEET THING

"God doesn't want something from us. He simply wants us."
— C.S. Lewis

MY BELOVED

The call to write this book felt clear to me, and I sincerely think this is a message God wants to give to his beloved daughters. I have been in prayer for some time over what His message would be to each of you, and this is what I felt He wanted you to know:

My Beloved,

Although you may not always perceive me, I am with you (Isaiah 41:10).

Before I made the world, I loved you and chose you to be holy and without fault (Ephesians 1:4).

I created you in My own image (Genesis 1:27).

I see you, and I know every detail about you down to the number of hairs on your head (Luke 12:7).

I knew you and set you apart before you were formed (Jeremiah 1:5).

I knit you in your mother's womb (Psalms 139:13).

You were created with a plan and purpose, and I have given you beautiful and specific gifts to fulfill those plans (Jeremiah 29:11).

I will equip you and lead you (Psalms 32:8).

You are valuable (Luke 12:24).

All your days are written in my book (Psalms 139:16).

Every good gift that you receive comes from my hand (James 1:17).

I want to lavish my love on you (1 John 3:1).

I rejoice over you with singing, and I treasure you (Zephaniah3:17/Exodus 19:5).

If you seek me with all your heart, you will find Me (Jeremiah 29:13).

If you ask Me, I will show you marvelous and wonderful things you could never figure out alone (Jeremiah 33:3).

I can do more for you than you can possibly imagine or think (Ephesians 3:20).

As you put your trust in me, I am directing your steps (Proverbs 16:9).

I sent my only Son to be sacrificed for the remission of your sins (Romans 8:31-32).

Jesus died so that you and I could be together (2 Corinthians 5:18-19).

In Him, my love for you is revealed (John 17:26).

If you receive the gift of my son Jesus, you receive Me (1 John 2:23).

I know you have suffered grief and many trials (John 16:33), and I have stored every tear (Psalm 56:8).

You have been broken-hearted, and I have been close to you (Psalm 34:18).

One day soon, I will wipe away every tear from your eyes, and I will take away all of the pain you have suffered (Rev 21:3-4).

We will have the biggest celebration in heaven! (Luke 15:7)

Remember My promises to you, My beautiful daughter, and who I have created you to be.

My Son will return (Rev 22:12).

I want all My beloved children to come home (1 Timothy 2:4-6).

Will you trust Me? Will you be My child? (John 1:12-13).

I am waiting for you (Luke 15:11-32).

Love,

Your heavenly Father

A WORD ABOUT THE AUTHOR

Julie Hedenborg feels grateful for her nursing career and is now enjoying this time with her family being mom. She loves giving God glory and managing the testimonies that come to her for the podcast. Everyday Miracles Podcast has been heard around the globe with over a million downloads.

- Free Christian meditations and affirmations: www.ChristianMeditationsForMoms.com
- How to contact Julie Hedenborg by email: julie@everydaymiraclespodcast.com
- Website: everydaymiraclespodcast.com
- Everyday Miracles Podcast is available on YouTube, Spotify, iTunes, Stitcher, iHeartRadio, and most podcast platforms.

THE BEST IS YET TO COME

1 Corinthians 2:9

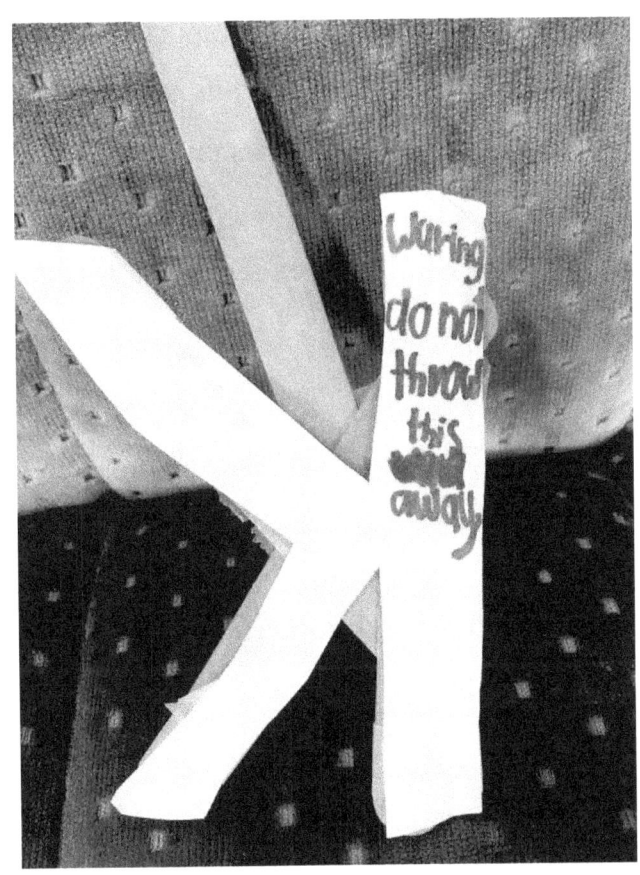

Art by Kendal Hedenborg

A FEW RESOURCES I WANT TO SHARE

That Have Grown My Faith or Blessed Me as A Mom

Jill Monaco's Hearing from God Challenge, mentorship, and workbook. The Freedom Coach Model: Encounter the Presence of God and Find Freedom in Christ Through Powerful Questions and Listening Prayers. CreateSpace Independent Publishing Platform, October 18, 2017.

Priscilla Shirer Armor of God Bible Study. Seven session study for Learning How to Prepare for the Attacks of the Enemy. Lifeway.com

Christine Caine Bible Study Unexpected, Leave Fear Behind, Move Forward in Faith and Embrace the Adventure. Lifeway.com

Kirk Martin of Celebrate Calm and the Calm Parenting Podcast has been an amazing Coach and blessing to my family. He has expertise with a variety of kids with special needs. www.celebratecalm.com

Havilah Cunnington Bible Study Discovering & Activating My Spiritual Gifts: A 15-Day Bible Study to Help you Identify and Understand your Unique Spiritual Gifts.

Lisa Harper's Kerygma Summit is a 3-day event to equip women in the areas of sound biblical exegesis, hermeneutics, and practical theology. See www.KerygmaSummit.com

Lisa Harper Back Porch Theology Podcast

Christine Caine Equip & Empower Podcast

Weekend to Remember Marriage Getaway events at www.familylife.com

Joyce Meyer Battlefield of the Mind, Winning the Battle in Your Mind Bible Study

Max Lucado Unshakable Hope Bible Study

Beth Moore Here and Now, There and Then, Study of Book of Revelation

NOTES

Holy Bible: New Living Translation. Wheaton, Ill: Tyndale House Publishers, 2004. Print.

The Bible. Good News Bible Version. YouVersion, app version 5.0, British & Foreign Bible Society, 1996.

1. The Social Dilemma Documentary. Directed by Jeff Orlowski, Produced by Exposure Labs, the Space Program, and Agent Pictures. 2020. Netflix.

2. Crist, Carolyn. "One-Week Social Media Break Reduces Anxiety, Depression." May 6, 2022, WebMD, LLC.

3. Bouygues, Helen Lee. "Social Media Is a Public Health Crisis. Let's Treat It Like One." US News. July 20, 2021, at 10:40 a.m.

4. Luke 2:45-46 When they couldn't find him, they went back to Jerusalem to search for him there. Three days later they finally discovered him in the Temple, sitting among the religious teachers, listening to them, and asking questions. (NLT)

5. Rosenberg, Jaime. "The Effects of Chronic Fear on a Person's Health." November 11, 2017. The American Journal of Managed Care.

6. National Academy of Sciences, Engineering and Medicine. 2020. Social Isolation and Loneliness in Older Adults: Opportunities for the Health Care System. Washington, DC: The National Academies Press.

7. Menges, Sara. "The 3 Biggest Advantages of Human Touch May Surprise You," PlushCare, Jan 24, 2021.

8. McLaren, Leah. "The Excruciating Loneliness of Being a New Mother," from Today's Parent Magazine. March 2018.

9. Dodds, Dr. Jodi A. and Anderson, Amanda P. Carotid and Vertebral Artery Dissection; A Guide for Survivors and Their Loved Ones, CCC-SLP, Sept 2017, Columbia, SC, CreateSpace Independent Publishing Platform, August 11, 2017,   page 121.

10. Amen Clinic, "What Social Isolation is Really Doing to Your Health," Amen Clinic Blog, July 30, 2020.

11. Monaco, Jill. The Freedom Coach Model: Encounter the Presence of God and Find Freedom in Christ Through Powerful Questions and Listening Prayers. CreateSpace Independent Publishing Platform, October 18, 2017.

12. Woodford, Jim. Heaven, An Unexpected Journey. Shippensburg, PA. Destiny Image, Aug 21, 2020.

13. Tabatt, Shaun. June 2, 2022, "College Kid Has Traumatic Brain Injury in Skateboard Accident and Encounters Jesus in Heaven," June 2, 2022, Interview with Host Shaun Tabatt and Gabe Poirot, Destiny Image. (minute 18:30).

14. Johnson, Ryan. June 20, 2022, "Real Near-Death Experience Stories," Blacksmith Chronicles Podcast interview, Guests Randy Kay and Shaun Tabatt, Episode, (minute 29).

15. John 10:10 The thief's purpose is to steal and kill and destroy. My purpose is to give them a rich and satisfying life. (NLT)

16. 2 Corinthians 11:14 But I am not surprised! Even Satan disguises himself as an angel of light. (NLT)

17. Pew Research Center, November 23, 2021, "Views on the afterlife." Washington, DC.

18. Hedenborg, Julie. August 18, 2021, "Imagine Heaven with Guest John Burke," Episode 73, Everyday Miracles Podcast (minute 9:15).

19. Burke, John. Imagine Heaven; Near Death Experiences, God's Promises, and the Exhilarating Future That Awaits You, Grand Rapids, Baker Books, 2015, page 31.

20. 2 Corinthians 10:5 We destroy every proud obstacle that keeps people from knowing God. We capture their rebellious thoughts and teach them to obey Christ. (NLT)

21. Gupta, Shreya. May 7, 2021. "We Decode the Science Behind Affirmations and How They can Infuse Positivity in Your Life." Health shots.

22. Moore, C. 2019 "Positive Daily Affirmations: Is There Science Behind It?" Positive Psychology.

23. Burke, John. Imagine Heaven; Near Death Experiences, God's Promises, and the Exhilarating Future That Awaits You, Grand Rapids, Baker Books, 2015. see pg. 317 Appendix A, "Reasons to Believe".

24. Evans, Jimmy. Tipping Point; The End is Here. Dallas, XO Publishing, 2020.

25. Atlas of Israel 1985 page 17, Fault line at mount olives corresponds with Zechariah 14:4 "On that day his feet will stand on the Mount of Olives, east of Jerusalem. And the Mount of Olives will split apart, making a wide valley running from east to west. Half the mountain will move toward the south." (NLT)

CAPTIONS/CREDIT FOR PHOTOGRAPHY

1. Front Cover Photo: Family fun with our photo shoot at Romare Bearden Park. *Credit Lindsay Hart.*

2. Page xv: Lindsay drapes us in a wool blanket while Lars is already dripping with sweat. Me realizing that his tolerance for this photo shoot is the purest expression of his love. *Credit Lindsay Hart.*

3. Comparison Photo, page 1: Kendal having fun with her silly Daddy on a family trip to Hilton Head.

4. Perfectionism Photo, page 11: Left: Our attempt at a family photo on the beach when the magic of magic hour had passed. Top right: Kendal proudly shares her potty-training work after a lengthy time investment. Bottom right: My failed attempt at doggie eggs over-easy.

5. Fear Photo, page 21: Lars shares his birthday dessert.

6. Isolation Collage, page 31: Top left: Grace Stewart hugging her mother, affectionately known as Maw. Bottom left: Anders lovingly hugs his dog. Top right: Kendal and Anders having fun during a photo shoot. *Credit Lindsay Hart.* Bottom right: Anders spontaneously hugs his little sister.

7. Self-Neglect Photo, page 47: Anders and Kendal at their grandfather's house in Kentucky.

8. Pulling It All Together Photo, page 74: Kendal being her beautiful, spirited self in a neighbor's costume.

9. One Last Sweet Thing Photo, page 87: Anders runs to get one last vacation treat before we catch the shuttle, which officially ends our vacation eating freedom.

10. About the Author headshot by *Michelle Cichelli of Angel Eye Portraits*, page 91.

11. Back Cover headshot by *Michelle Cichelli of Angel Eye Portraits*.

www.ingramcontent.com/pod-product-compliance
Lightning Source LLC
Chambersburg PA
CBHW082109120626

46553CB00011B/3603